My Family / Mi familia

My Mom
Mi mamá

Thessaly Catt

PowerKids press & Editorial Buenas Letras
New York

To Riley and Kenny's mom, my sister Missy

Published in 2011 by The Rosen Publishing Group, Inc.
29 East 21st Street, New York, NY 10010

Copyright © 2011 by The Rosen Publishing Group, Inc.

All rights reserved. No part of this book may be reproduced in any form without permission in writing from the publisher, except by a reviewer.

First Edition

Editor: Maggie Murphy
Book Design: Ashley Burrell
Photo Researcher: Jessica Gerweck
Spanish translation: Eduardo Alamán

Photo Credits: Cover Jupiterimages/Getty Images; p. 5 Camille Tokerud/Getty Images; pp. 7 (mom, dad), 11, 12–13, 14, 18–19 Shutterstock.com; p. 7 (brother) © www.iStockphoto.com/Ekaterina Monakhova; p. 7 (sister) © www.iStockphoto.com/quavondo; p. 8 Ron Levine/Getty Images; p. 17 Image Source/Getty Images; p. 21 © www.iStockphoto.com/Catherine Yeulet; p. 22 © www.iStockphoto.com/Aldo Murillo.

Library of Congress Cataloging-in-Publication Data

Catt, Thessaly.
  My mom = Mi mamá / Thessaly Catt. — 1st ed.
    p. cm. — (My family = Mi familia)
  English and Spanish.
  Includes index.
  ISBN 978-1-4488-0717-8 (library binding)
  1. Mothers—Juvenile literature. 2. Mother and child—Juvenile literature. I. Title. II. Title: Mi mamá.
  HQ759.C298 2011b
  306.874'3—dc22

2010007494

Manufactured in the United States of America

CPSIA Compliance Information: Batch #WS10PK: For Further Information contact Rosen Publishing, New York, New York at 1-800-237-9932

Web Sites: Due to the changing nature of Internet links, PowerKids Press and Editorial Buenas Letras have developed an online list of Web sites related to the subject of this book. This site is updated regularly. Please use this link to access the list: www.powerkidslinks.com/family/mom/

Contents / Contenido

What Do Mothers Do?........................4
You and Your Mother.......................10
Learning About Families 16
Words to Know 24
Index 24

¿Qué hacen las mamás? 4
Tú y tu mamá 10
Aprendiendo sobre la familia 16
Palabras que debes saber..................24
Índice 24

Ricky and his mom are part of a family. Families are very important in Latin American **culture**.

Ricky y su mamá son parte de una familia. Las familias son muy importantes en la **cultura** de Latinoamérica.

This is a family tree. It shows the members of a family.

Éste es un árbol genealógico en el que vemos a los miembros de una familia.

Family Tree / Árbol genealógico

Dad / Papá

Mom / Mamá

Brother / Hermano

Sister / Hermana

Moms do all kinds of jobs. Mrs. Pérez builds houses. What does your mom do?

Las mamás hacen todo tipo de trabajos. La Sra. Pérez construye casas. ¿Qué hace tu mamá?

Kim's mom helps her when she gets hurt. Moms take good care of their kids.

La mamá de Kim le ayuda cuando se lastima. Las mamás cuidan muy bien a sus hijos.

Sara and Michael's mom helps them with their homework.

La mamá de Sara y Miguel les ayuda a hacer su tarea.

Cooking with your mom is fun! What do you like to do with your mom?

¡Cocinar con tu mamá es divertido! ¿Qué te gusta hacer con tu mamá?

All families are different. John's mother **adopted** him when he was a baby.

Todas las familias son diferentes. La mamá de Juan lo **adoptó** cuando era un bebé.

Dan and Nick's family took a trip to Mexico. Their mom taught them about her culture there.

La familia de Daniel y Nicolás viajó a México. Su mamá les habló de la cultura de este país.

Lucy and Maria sing "Happy Birthday" to their mom. Which holidays do you spend with your mom?

Lucía y María cantan "Feliz cumpleaños" a su mamá. Y tú, ¿qué fiestas pasas con tu mamá?

Your family loves you. Your mom is a big part of your family!

Tu familia te quiere mucho. ¡Tu mamá es parte muy importante de tu familia!

Words to Know / Palabras que debes saber

adopted (uh-DOPT-ed) Made a child born to another mother part of one's family.

culture (KUL-chur) The beliefs, practices, and arts of a group of people.

---

adoptar Hacer parte de tu familia a un niño o niña nacido en otra familia.

cultura (la) Las creencias, prácticas y artes de un grupo de personas.

Index

B
baby, 16
birthday, 20

C
culture, 4, 18

M
members, 6

Índice

B
bebé, 16

C
cultura, 4, 18
cumpleaños, 20

M
miembros, 6